BRITISH POETS SERIES

William Shakespeare: *Selected Sonnets and Verse*
edited, with an introduction by Mark Tuley

Edmund Spenser: *Poems*
selected and introduced by Teresa Page

Robert Herrick: *Selected Poems*
edited and introduced by M.K. Pace

John Donne: *Poems*
selected and introduced by A.H. Ninham

D.H. Lawrence: *Selected Poems*
edited with an introduction by Margaret Elvy

Percy Bysshe Shelley: *Poems*
selected and introduced by Charlotte Greene

Sir Thomas Wyatt: *Love For Love: Selected Poems*
edited by Louise Cooper

Thomas Hardy: *Selected Poems*
edited, with an introduction by A.H. Ninham

Emily Bronte: *Poems*
selected and introduced by Teresa Page

John Keats: *Selected Poems*
edited with an introduction by Miriam Chalk

Henry Vaughan: *Poems*
selected and introduced by A.H. Ninham

The Crescent Moon Book of Mystical Poetry in English
edited by Carol Appleby

The Crescent Moon Book of Nature Poetry From Langland to Lawrence
edited by Margaret Elvy

The Crescent Moon Book of Metaphysical Poetry
edited and introduced by Charlotte Greene

The Crescent Moon Book of Elizabethan Love Poetry
edited and introduced by Carol Appleby

The Crescent Moon Book of Romantic Poetry
edited and introduced by L.M. Poole

Blinded By Her Light The Love-Poetry of Robert Graves
by Jeremy Robinson

The Best of Peter Redgrove's Poetry: The Book of Wonders
by Peter Redgrove, edited and introduced by Jeremy Robinson

Peter Redgrove: Here Comes the Flood
by Jeremy Robinson

Sex-Magic-Poetry-Cornwall: A Flood of Poems
by Peter Redgrove, edited with an essay by Jeremy Robinson

Brigitte's Blue Heart
by Jeremy Reed

Claudia Schiffer's Red Shoes
by Jeremy Reed

By-Blows: Uncollected Poems
by D.J. Enright

Shakespeare: Love, Poetry and Magic
in Shakespeare's Sonnets and Plays
by B.D. Barnacle

The Crescent Moon Book of Love Poetry

The Crescent Moon Book of
Love Poetry

Edited by Louise Cooper

CRESCENT MOON

CRESCENT MOON PUBLISHING
P.O. Box 1312, Maidstone
Kent, ME14 5XU
Great Britain
www.crmoon.com

First published 1994. Second edition 2008. Third edition 2016.
Introduction © Louise Cooper, 1994, 2008, 2016.

Printed and bound in the U.S.A.
Set in Garamond Book 10 on 12pt.
Designed by Radiance Graphics.

British Library Cataloguing in Publication data

Crescent Moon Book of Love Poetry
I. Cooper, Louise
821.009354

ISBN-13 9781861711331
ISBN-13 9781861715272

Contents

ANONYMOUS
(13th century)

"Love is soft, love is swete"

Love is soft, love is swete, love is good sware;
Love is muche tene, love is muchel care.
Love is blissene mest, love is bot yare;
Love is wondred and wo with for to fare.

Love is hap, who it haveth; love is good hele.
Love is lecher and lees, and leef for to tele.
Love is doughty in the world with for to dele.
Love maketh in the land many unlede.

Love is stalwarde and strong to striden on stede.
Love is loveliche a thing to womane nede.
Love is hardy and hot as glowinde glede.
Love maketh many may with teres to wede.

Love hath his stward by sty and by strete.
Love maketh many may hire wonges to wete.
Love is hap, who it haveth, on for to hete.
Love is wis, love is war, and wilful ansete.

Love is the sofeste thing in herte may slepe.
Love is craft, love is good with cares to kepe.

Love is lees, love is leef, love islonginge.
Love is fol, love is fast, love is frovringe.
Love is sellich an thing, whoso shal sooth singe.

Love is is wele, love is wo, love is gladhede.
Love is life, love is deth, love may us fede.

Were love all so londdrey as he is first kene,
It were the wordlokste thing in worlde were, ich wene.

It is y-said in an song, sooth is y-sene,
Love comseth with care and endeth with tene,
Mid lavedy, mid wive, mid maide, mid quene.

ANONYMOUS

(c. 1275)

"I sigh when I sing"

I sike al when I singe
   For sorwe that I see,
When ich with wepinge
   Biholde upon the tree:
I see Jesu, my swete,
His herte-blood forlete
   For the love of me;
His woundes waxen wete.
Marie, milde and swete,
   Thou haf mercy of me!

Hey upon a downe,
   As al folk it see may,
A mile without the towne,
   Aboute the mid-day,
The roode was up arerde.
His friendes weren of-ferde:
   They clungen so the clay.
The roode stont in ston;
Mary herself alon –
   Her song was way-la-way.

When ich Him biholde
   With ey and herte bo,
I see His body colde;
   His blee waxeth al blo.
He hangeth al of bloode
So hey upon the roode
   Bitwixen theves two.
How should I singe more?
Mary, thou wepe sore,
   Thou wist al of his wo.

Wel ofte when I sike,
   I make my mon;
Ivel it may me like –
   And wonder n'is it non –
When I see hange hey
And bitter paines drey
   Jesu my lemmon.
His woundes sore smerte;
The sper is at His herte
   And thurgh His side gon.

The nailes beeth al to stronge,
   The smith is al to sleye;
Thou bledes al to longe,
   The tree is al to heye.
The stones waxen wete –
Allas! jesu, my swete,
   Few frends hafdes neye,
But Sein jon murnind
And Mary wepind,
   That al thy sorwe seye.

Wel ofte when I slepe
   With sorwe ich am thurgh-soght;
When I wake I wepe,
   I thenke in my thoght:
Allas! that men beeth woode,
Biholdeth on the roode
   And seleth – ich ly noght –
Her soules into in
For any worldes win,
   That was so dere y-boght!

ANONYMOUS

(14th century)

A Maid Mars Me

With longing I am lad,
On molde I waxe mad:
   A maide marreth me.
I grede, grone unglad;
For selden I am sad
   That seemly for to see
   Levedy, thou rewe me!
To routhe thou havest me rad;
Be bote of that I bad;
      My lif is long on thee.

Levedy of alle londe,
Les me out of bonde;
   Brought ich am in wo.
Have resting on honde
And send thou me thy sonde
   Soone, er thou me slo;
   My rest is with the ro.
Though men to me han onde,
To love n'il I nought wonde
      Ne lete for non of tho.

Levedy, with al my might
My love is on thee light,
   To menske when I may,
Thou rew and reed me right.
To dethe thou havest me dight:
   I deye thou havest me dight:
   I deye longe er my day –
   Thou leve upon my lay.
Treuthe ich have thee plight
To don that ich have hight
      Whil my lif laste may.

Lilie-whit heo is,
Hir rode so rose on ris,
   That reveth me my rest.
Womman war and wis,
Of pride heo bereth the pris,
   Burde one of the best,
   This womman woneth by west,
Brightest under bis;
Heven I tolde al his
      That to night were hir gest.

JOHN SKELTON

(c. 1460-1529)

"Merry Margaret"

Merry Margaret, as midsummer flower,
Gentle as falcon or hawk of the tower,
With solace and gladness,
Much mirth and no madness,
All good and no badness;
So joyously,
So maidenly,
So womanly,
Her demeaning;
In every thing
Far far passing
That I can indite
Or suffice to write
Of merry Margaret, as midsummer flower,
Gentle as falcon or hawk of the tower.
As patient and as still,
And as full of good will,
As the fair Isyphill,
Coliander,
Sweet pomander,
Good Cassander;
Steadfast of thought,
Well made, well wrought.
Far may be sought
Erst than ye can find
So courteous, so kind,
As merry Margaret, the midsummer flower,
Gentle as falcon or hawk of the tower.

SIR THOMAS WYATT

(1503-1542)

"My heart I gave thee"

My heart I gave thee, not to do it pain;
But to preserve, it was to thee taken.
I served thee, not to be forsaken,
But that I should be rewarded again.
I was content thy servant to remain
But not to be paid under this fashion.
Now since in thee is none other reason,
Displease thee not if that I do refrain,
Unsatiate of my woe and thy desire,
Assured by craft to excuse thy fault.
But since it please thee to feign a default,
Farewell, I say, parting from the fire:
For he that believeth bearing in hand,
Plougeth in water and soweth in the sand.

"What means this when I lie alone?"

What means this when I lie alone?
I toss, I turn, I sigh, I groan.
My bed me seems as hard as stone.
    What means this?

I sigh, I plain continually.
The clothes that on my bed do lie
Always methink they lie awry.
    What means this?

In slumbers oft for fear I quake.
For heat and cold I burn and shake.
For lack of sleep my head doth ache.
    What means this?

A mornings then when I do rise
I turn unto my wonted guise,
All day after muse and devise.
    What means this?

And if perchance by me there pass
She unto whom I sue for grace,
The cold blood forsaketh my face.
    What means this?

But if I sit near her by
With loud voice my heart doth cry
And yet my mouth is dumb and dry.
    What means this?

To ask for help no heart I have.
My tongue doth fail what I should crave.
Yet inwardly I rage and rave.
    What means this?

Thus have I passed many year
And many a day, though naught appear
But most of that that most I fear.
    What means this?

"Go, burning sighs"

Go, burning sighs, unto the frozen heart.
Go break the ice which pity's painful dart
Might never pierce; and if mortal prayer
In heaven may be heard, at last I desire
That death or mercy be end of my smart.
Take with thee pain whereof I have my part
And eke the flame from which I cannot start,
And leave me then in rest, I you require.
  Go, burning sighs.
I must go work, I see, by craft and art
For truth and faith in her is laid apart.
Alas, I cannot therefore assail her
With pitiful plaint and scalding fire
That out of my breast doth strainly start.
  Go, burning sighs.

"I find no peace"

I find no peace and all my war is done.
I fear and hope, I burn and freeze like ice.
I fly above the wind yet can I not arise.
And naught I have and all the world I seize on.
That looseth nor locketh, holdeth me in prison
And holdeth me not, yet can I scape no wise;
Nor letteth me live nor die at my device
And yet of death it giveth me occasion.
Without eyen I see and without tongue I plain.
I desire to perish and yet I ask health.
I love another and thus I hate myself.
I feed me in sorrow and laugh in all my pain.
Likewise displeaseth me both death and life,
And my delight is causer of this strife.

"It burneth yet"

Lover: It burneth yet, alas, my heart's desire.
Lady:What is the thing that hath inflamed thy heart?
Lover: A certain point, as fervent as the fire.
Lady:The heat shall cease if that thou wilt convert.
Lover: I cannot stop the fervent raging ire.
Lady:What may I do if thyself cause thy smart?
Lover: Hear my request and rue my weeping cheer.
Lady: With right good will. Say on. Lo, I thee hear.

Lover: That thing would I maketh two content.
Lady:Thou seekest, perchance, of me that I may not.
Lover: Would God thou wouldst, as thou mayst
        well, assent.
Lady: That I may not. Thy grief is mine, God wot.
Lover: But I it feel, whatso thy words have meant.
Lady:Suspect me not. My words be not forgot.
Lover: Then say, alas, shall I have help or no?
Lady: I see no time to answer. Yea. But no.

Lover: Say yea, dear heart, and stand no more in doubt.
Lady:I may not grant a thing that is so dear.
Lover: Lo, with delays thou drives me still about.
Lady:Thou wouldest my death. It plainly doth appear.
Lover: First may my heart his blood and life bleed out.
Lady:Then for my sake, alas, thy will forbear.
Lover: From day to day thus wastes my life away.
Lady:Yet, for the best, suffer some small delay.

Lover: Now, good, say yea. Do once so good a deed.
Lady: If I said yea, what should thereof ensue?
Lover: An heart in pain, of succour so should speed.
    'Twixt yea and nay my doubt shall still renew.
    My sweet, say yea and do away this dread.
Lady:Thou wilt needs so. Be it so. But then be true.
Lover: Naught would I else, nor other treasure none.

Thus hearts be won by love, request, and moan.

QUEEN ELIZABETH I
(1533-1603)

On Monsieur's Departure

I grieve and dare not show my discontent,
I love and yet am forced to seem to hate,
I do, yet dare not say I ever meant,
I seem stark mute but inwardly do pate.
   I am and am not, I freeze and yet am burned,
   Since from myself another self I turned.

My care is like my shadow in the sun,
Follows me flying, flies when I pursue it,
Stands and lies by me, doth what I have done.
His too familiar care doth make me rue it.
   No means I find to rid him from my breast,
   Till by the end of things it be suppressed.

Some gentler passion slide into my mind,
For I am soft and made of melting snow;
Or be more cruel, love, and so be kind.
Let me float or sink, be high or low.
   Or let me live with some more sweet content,
   Or die and so forget what love e'er meant.

ANONYMOUS

(published 1597)

"Come away, come, sweet love"

Come away, come, sweet love,
The golden morning breaks,
All the earth, all the air
Of love and pleasure speaks,
Teach thine arms then to embrace,
And sweet rosy lips to kiss,
And mix our souls in mutual bliss,
Eyes were made for beauty's grace,
Viewing, rueing love's long pain,
Procur'd by beauty's rude disdain.

Come away, come, sweet love,
The golden morning wastes,
While the sun from his sphere
His fiery arrows casts:
Making all the shadows fly,
Playing, staying in the grove,
To entertain the stealth of love,
Thither, sweet love, let us hie,
Flying, dying, in desire,
Wing'd with sweet hopes and heav'nly fire.

Come away, come, sweet love,
Do not in vain adorn
Beauty's grace that should rise
Like to the naked morn:
Lilies on the river's side,
And fair cyprian flowers new blown,
Desire no beauties but their own,
Ornament is nurse of pride,
Pleasure, measure, love's delight,
Haste then, sweet love, our wished flight.

EDMUND SPENSER

(1552?-1599)

from Amoretti

III

The soverayne beauty which I do admyre,
Witnesse the world how worthy to be prayzed!
The light wherof hath kindled heavenly fyre
In my fraile spirit, by her from basenesse raysed;
That being now with her huge brightnesse dazed,
Base thing I can no more endure to view:
But, looking still on her, I stand amazed
At wondrous sight of so celestiall hew.
So when my toung would speak her praises dew,
It stopped is with thoughts astonishment;
And when my pen would write her titles true,
It ravisht is with fancies wonderment:
  Yet in my hart I then both speak and write
  The wonder that my wit cannot endite.

VII

Fayre eyes! the myrrour of my mazed hart,
What wondrous vertue is contayn'd in you,
The which both lyfe and death forth from you dart
Into the obiect of your mighty view?
For when ye mildly looke with lovely hew,
Then is my soule with life and love inspired:
But when ye lowre, or looke on me askew,
Then do I die, as one with lightning fyred.
But since that lyfe is more then death desyred,
Looke ever lovely, as becomes you best;
That your bright beams, of my weak eyes admyred,
May kindle living fire within my brest.
    Such life should be the honor of your light,
    Such death the sad ensample of your might.

XVII

The glorious pourtraict of that angels face,
Made to amaze weake mens confused skil,
And this worlds worthlesse glory to embase,
What pen, what pencil!, can expresse her fill?
For though he colours could devize at will,
And eke his learned hand at pleasure guide,
Least, trembling, it his workmanship should spill,
Yet many wondrous things there are beside:
The sweet eye-glaunces, that like arrowes glide,
The charming smiles, that rob sence from the hart,
The lovely pleasance, and the lofty pride,
Cannot expressed be by any art.
　A greater craftesmans hand thereto doth neede,
　That can expresse the life of things indeed.

XXX

My Love is lyke to yse, and I to fyre:
How comes it then that this her cold so great
Is not dissolv'd through my so hot desyre,
But harder growes the more I her intreat?
Or how comes it that my exceeding heat
Is not delayd by her hart-frosen cold,
But that I burne much more in boyling sweat,
And feele my flames augmented manifold?
What more miraculous thing may be told,
That fire, which all things melts, should harden yse,
And yse, which is congeald with sencelesse cold,
Should kindle fyre by wonderful devyse?
    Such is the powre of love in gentle mind,
    That it can alter all the course of kynd.

XXXIX

Sweet smile! the daughter of the Queene of Love,
Expressing all thy mothers powrefull art,
With which she wonts to temper angry Iove,
When all the gods he threats with thundring dart,
Sweet is thy vertue, as thy selfe sweet art.
For when on me thou shinedst late in sadnesse,
A melting pleasance ran through every part,
And me revived with hart-robbing gladnesse;
Whylest rapt with joy resembling heavenly madness,
My soule was ravisht quite as in a traunce,
And, feeling thence no more her sorrowes sadnesse,
Fed on the fulnesse of that chearfull glaunce.
  More sweet than nectar, or ambrosiall meat,
  Seem'd every bit which thenceforth I did eat.

SIR PHILIP SIDNEY

(1554-1586)

"O my thoughts's sweet food"

O my thoughts's sweet food, my, my only owner,
  O my heavens for taste by heavenly pleasure,
Of the fair nymph born to do women honour,
                    Lady my Treasure.

Where be now those joys, that I lately tasted?
  Where be now those eyes ever inly persers?
Where be now those worlds never idly wasted,
                    Wounds to rehearsers?

Where is ah that face, that a sun defaces?
  Where be those welcomes by no worth deserved?
Where be those movings, the delights, the graces?
                    How be we swerved?

O hideous absence, by thee am I thralled.
  O my vain word gone, ruin of my glory.
O due allegiance, by thee am I called
                    Still to be sorry.

But no more words, though words be spoken,
  Nor no more wording with a word to spill me.
Peace, due allegiance, duty must be broken,
                    If duty kill me.

Then come, O come, then I do come, receive me,
  Slay me not, for stay do not hide thy blisses,
But between those arms, never else do leave me;
                    Give my thy kisses.

O my thoughts' sweet food, my, my only owner,
  O my heavens for taste, by thy heavenly pleasure,
O the fair nymph born to do women honour,
                    Lady my Treasure.

from Sonnets of Astrophel and Stella

In nature, apt to like, when I did see
   Beauties which were of many carrets fine,
My boiling sprites did thither then incline,
And, Love, I thought that I was full of thee:
But finding not those restlesse flames in mee,
   Which others said did make their souls to pine,
   I thought those babes of some pinnes hurt did whine,
By my soul iudging what Loves paine might be.
But while I thus with this young lion plaid,
   Mine eyes (shall I say curst or blest?) beheld
Stella: now she is nam'd, neede more be said?
   In her sight I a lesson new haue speld.
     I now haue learnd love right, and learnd euen so
     As they that being poysond poyson know.

"I might (unhappy words!)"

I might (unhappy word!) O me, I might,
   And then I would not, or could not, see my blisse,
Till now wrapt in a most infernall night,
I find how heau'nly day, wretch! I did misse.
Hart, rend thyself, thou dost thyself but right;
   No lovely Paris made thy Hellen his;
   No force, no fraud robd thee of thy delight,
Nor Fortune of thy fortune author is,
But to my selfe my selfe did giue the blow,
   While too much wit, forsooth, so troubled me
That I respects for both our sakes must show:
   And yet could not, by rysing morne fore-see
     How fair a day was near: O punisht eyes,
     That I had bene more foolish, or more wise!

"Stella, the only planet"

Stella, the only planet of my light,
   Light of my life, and life of my desire,
Chief good whereto my hope doth only aspire,
World of my wealth, and heaven of my delight,
Why dost thou spend the treasures of thy spright,
   With voice more fit to wed Amphion's lyre,
   Seeking to quench in me the noble fire
Fed by thy worth, and kindled by thy sight?
And all in vain; for while thy breath most sweet
   With choicest words, thy words with reasons rare,
Thy reasons firmly set on Virtue's feet,
   Labour to kill in me this killing care,
     O think I then, what paradise of joy
     It is, so fair a virtue to enjoy!

GEORGE CHAPMAN

(1559?-1634)

Epithalamion Teratos

Come, come, dear Night, Love's mart of kisses,
Sweet close of his ambitious line,
The fruitful summer of his blisses,
Love's glory doth in darkness shine.
O come, soft rest of cares, come Night,
Come naked Virtue's only tire,
The reaped harvest of the light,.
Bound up in sheaves of sacred fire.
  Love calls to war,
  Sighs his alarms,
  Lips his swords are,
  The field his arms.
Come, Night, and lay thy velvet hand
On glorious Day's outfacing face,
And all thy crowned flames command
For torches to our nuptial grace.
  Love calls to war,
  Sighs his alarms,
  Lips his swords are,
  The field his arms.
No need have we of factious Day,
To cast in envy of thy peace
Her balls of discord in thy way:
Here Beauty's day doth never cease;
Day is abstracted here,
And varied in a triple sphere.
Hero, Alcame, Mya outshine thee,
Ere thou come here let Thetis thrice refine thee.
  Love calls to war,
  Sighs his alarms,
  Lips his swords are,
  The field his arms.
The evening star I see:
Rise, youths, the evening star
Helps Love to summon war;
Both now embracing be.

Rise, youths, Love's right claims more than banquets, rise.
Now the bright marigolds that deck the skies,
Phoebus' celestial flowers, that (contrary
To his flowers here) ope when he shuts his eye,
And shut when he doth open, crown your sports.
Now Love in Night, and Night in love exhorts
Courtship and dances. All your parts employ,
And suit Night's rich expansure with your joy.
Love paints his longings in sweet virgins' eyes:
Rise, youths, Love's right claims more than banquets, rise.
Rise, virgins, let fair nuptial love enfold
Your fruitless breasts: the maidenheads ye hold
Are not your own alone, but parted are;
Part in disposing them your parents share,
And that a third part is, so must ye save
Your loves a third, and you your thirds must have.
Love paints his longings in sweet virgins' eyes:
Rise, youths, love's right claims more than banquets, rise.

SAMUEL DANIEL

(1562-1619)

from Sonnets to Delia

Fair is my Love, and cruel as she's fair
   Her brow shades frowns, although her eyes are sunny;
Her smiles are lightning, though her pride despair;
   And her disdains are gall, her favours honey.
A modest maid, decked with a blush of honour,
   Whose feet to tread green paths of youth and love,
The wonder of all eyes that look upon her,
   Sacred on earth, designed a saint above!
Chastity and Beauty, which were deadly foes,
   Live reconciled friends within her brow;
And had the Pity to conjoin with those,
   Then who had heard the plaints I utter now?
     For had she not been fair, and thus unkind,
     My Muse had slept, and none had known my mind.

"For had she not been fair"

For had she not been fair and thus unkind,
   Then had no finger pointed at my lightness;
The world had never known what I do find,
   And clouds obscure had shaded still her brightness.
Then had no censor's eye these lines surveyed,
   Nor graver brows have judged my Muse so vain;
No sun my blush and error had bewrayed,
   Nor yet the world had heard of such disdain.
Then had I walked with bold erected face;
   No downcast look had signified my miss;
But my degraded hopes with such disgrace
   Did force me groan out griefs and utter this.
     For being full, should I not then have spoken,
     My sense oppressed had failed and heart had broken.

"If this be love"

If this be love, to draw a weary breath,
    To paint on floods till the shore cry to th'air;
With downward looks still reading on the earth.
    These sad memorials of my love's despair;
If this be love, to war against my soul,
    Lie down to wail, rise up to sigh and grieve,
The never-resting stone of care to roll,
    Still to complain my griefs, whilst none relieve;
If this be love, to clothe me with dark thoughts,
    Haunting untrodden paths to wail apart,
My pleasures horror, music tragic notes,
    Tears in mine eyes and sorrow at my heart;
        If this be love, to live a living death,
        Then do I love, and draw this weary breath.

HENRY CONSTABLE
(1562-1613)

from Sonnets to Diana

To live in hell, and heaven to behold;
  To welcome life, and die a living death;
To sweat with heat, and yet be freezing cold;
  To grasp at stars, and lie the earth beneath;
To tread a maze that never shall have end;
  To burn in sighs, and starve in daily tears;
To climb a hill, and never to descend;
  Giants to kill, and quake at childish fears;
To pine for food, and watch th' Hesperides tree;
  To thirst for drink, and nectar still to draw;
To live accursed, women, hold blest to be,
    And weep those wrongs which never creature saw:
      If this be love, if love in these be founded,
      My heart is love, for these in it are grounded.

IV

Of her excellency both in singing and instruments

Not that thy hand is soft, is sweet, is white,
    Thy lips sweet roses, breast sweet lily is,
That love esteems these three the chiefest bliss
    Which nature ever made for lips' delight;
But when these three to show their heavenly might
    Such wonders do, devotion then for this
Commandeth us with humble zeal to kiss
    Such things as work miracles in our sight.
A lute of senseless wood, by nature dumb,
    Touched by thy hand doth speak divinely well;
And from thy lips and breast sweet tunes do come
    To my dead heart, the which new life do give.
      Of greater wonders heard we never tell
      Than for the dumb to speak, the dead to live.

VII

Complaint of misfortune in love only

Now, now I love indeed, and suffer more
  In one day now then I did in a year;
Great flames they be which but small sparkles were,
  And wounded now, I was but pricked before.
No marvel then, though more than heretofore
  I weep and sigh; how can great wounds be there
Where moisture runs not out? and ever, where
  The fire is great, of smoke there must be store.
My heart was hitherto but like green wood,
  Which must be dried before it will burn bright;
My former love served but my heart to dry;
  Now Cupid for his fire doth find it good:
    For now it burneth clear, and shall give light
    For all the world your beauty to espy.

MICHAEL DRAYTON
(1563-1631)

"So well I love thee"

So well I love thee, as without thee I
Love nothing; if I might choose, I'd rather die
Than be one day debarr'd thy company.

Since beasts, and plants do grow, and live and move,
Beasts are those men, that such a life approve:
He only lives, that deadly is in love.

The corn that in the ground is sown first dies
And of one seed do many ears arise:
Love, this world's corn, by dying multiplies.

The seeds of love first by thy eyes were thrown
Into a ground untill'd, a heart unknown
To bear such fruit, till by thy hands 'twas sown.

Look as your looking-glass by chance may fall,
Divide and break in many pieces small
And yet shows forth the selfsame face in all:

Proportions, features, graces just the same,
And in the smallest piece as well the name
Of fairest one deserves, as in the richest frame.

So all my thoughts are pieces but of you
Which put together makes a glass so true
As I therein no other's face but yours can view.

from Idea

"An evil spirit, your beauty, haunts me still"

An evil spirit, your beauty, haunts me still,
  Wherewith (alas) I have been long possessed,
Which ceaseth not to tempt me to each ill,
  Nor gives me once but one poor minute's rest.
In me it speaks, whether I sleep or wake,
  And when by means to drive it out I try,
With greater torments then it me doth take,
  And tortures me in most extremity.
Before my face it lays down my despairs,
  And hastes me on unto a sudden death,
Now tempting me to drown myself in tears,
  And then in sighing to give up my breath.
    Thus am I still provoked to every evil
    By this good wicked spirit, sweet angel devil.

"Since there's no help"

Since there's no help, come let us kiss and part,
Nay, I have done: you get no more of me,
And I am glad, yea, glad with all my heart,
That thus so cleanly I myself can free,
Shake hands for ever, cancel all our vows,
And when we meet at any time again,
Be it not seen in either of our brows,
That we one jot of former love retain;
Now at the last gasp, of love's latest breath,
When, his pulse failing, passion speechless lies,
When faith is kneeling by his bed of death,
And innocence is closing up his eyes,
   Now if thou would'st, when all have given him over,
   From death to life, thou might'st him yet recover.

CHRISTOPHER MARLOWE
(1564-1593)

The Passionate Sheepheard to His Love

Come live with me, and be my love,
And we will all the pleasure prove,
That Valleys, groves, hills and fields,
Woods, or steepy mountain yields.

And we will sit upon the Rocks,
Seeing the Shepherds feed their flocks,
By shallow Rivers, to whose falls,
Melodious birds sing Madrigalls.

And I will make thee beds of Roses,
And a thousand fragrant poesies,
A cap of flowers, and a kirtle,
Embroidered all with leaves of Myrtle.

A gown made of the finest wool,
Which from our pretty Lambs we pull,
Fair lined slippers for the cold:
With buckles of the purest gold.

A belt of straw, and Ivy buds,
With Coral clasps and Amber studs,
And if these pleasures may thee move,
Come live with me, and be my love.

The Shepherds Swains shall dance and sing,
For thy delight each May morning,
If these delights thy mind may move;
Then live with me, and be my love.

WILLIAM SHAKESPEARE
(1564-1616)

from *The Sonnets*

18

Shall I compare thee to a summer's day?
Thou art more lovely and more temperate:
Rough winds do shake the darling buds of May,
And summer's lease hath all too short a date:
Sometimes too hot the eye of heaven shines,
And often is his gold complexion dimm'd,
And every fair from fair sometime declines,
By chance or nature's changing course untrimm'd:
But thy eternal summer shall not fade
Nor lose possession of that fair thou ow'st,
Nor shall Death brag thou wander'st in his shade,
When in eternal lines to time thou grow'st:
    So long as men can breathe or eyes can see,
    So long lives this, and this gives life to thee.

20

A woman's face with nature's own hand painted
Hast thou, the master-mistress of my passion;
A woman's gentle heart, but not acquainted
With shifting change as is false women's fashion;
An eye more bright than theirs, less false in rolling,
Gilding the object whereupon it gazeth;
A man in hue all hues in so controlling,
Which steals men's eyes and women's souls amazeth:
And for a woman wert thou first created, –
Till nature as she wrought thee fell a-doting,
And by addition me of thee defeated,
By adding one thing to my purpose nothing.
    But since she prick'd thee out for women's pleasure,
    Mine be thy love and thy love's use their pleasure.

40

Take all my loves, my love, yea, take them all:
What hast thou then more than thou hadst before?
No love, my love, that thou mayst true love call –
All mine was thine, before thou hadst this more.
Then if for my love thou my love receivest,
I cannot blame thee, for my love thou usest, –
But yet be blam'd, if thou this self deceivest
By wilful taste of what thy self refusest.
I do forgive thy robbery, gentle thief,
Although thou steal thee all my poverty:
And yet love knows it is a greater grief
To bear love's wrong than hate's knowing injury.
    Lascivious grave, in whom all ill well shows,
    Kill me with spites, yet we must not be foes.

56

Sweet love, renew thy force; be it not said
Thy edge should blunter be than appetite,
Which but today by feeding is allay'd,
Tomorrow sharpen'd in his former might:
So, love, be thou; although today thou fill
Thy hungry eyes even till they wink with fulness,
Tomorrow see again, and do not kill
The spirit of love with a perpetual dulness:
Let this sad interim like the ocean be
Which parts the shore where two contracted new
Come daily to the banks, that when they see
Return of love more blest may be the view:
    As call it winter, which being full of care
    Makes summer's welcome, thrice more wish'd, more rare.

104

To me, fair friend, you can never be old,
For as you were when first your eye I eyed
Such seems your beauty still: three winters cold
Have from the forests shook three summer's pride,
Three beauteous springs to yellow autumn turn'd
In process of the seasons have I seen,
Three April perfumes in three hot Junes burn'd,
Since first I saw you fresh which yet are green.
Ah yet doth beauty like a dial hand
Steal from his figure and no pace perceiv'd,
So your sweet hue, which methinks still doth stand,
Hath motion, and mine eye may be deceiv'd,
    For fear of which hear this, thou age unbred:
    Ere you were born was beauty's summer dead.

116

Let me not to the marriage of true minds
Admit impediments: love is not love
Which alters when it alteration finds,
Or bends with the remover to remove.
Oh no! it is an ever-fixed mark
That looks on tempests and is never shaken;
It is the star to every wandering bark,
Whose worth's unknown although his height be taken.
Love's not Time's fool, though rosy lips and cheeks
Within his bending sickle's compass come;
Love alters not with his brief hours and weeks,
But bears it out even to the edge of doom.
    If this be error and upon me prov'd,
    I never writ, nor no man ever lov'd.

129

The expense of spirit in a waste of shame
Is lust in action; and till action, lust
Is perjur'd, murderous, bloody, full of blame,
Savage, extreme, rude, cruel, not to trust;
Enjoy'd no sooner but despised straight;
Past reason hunted; and no sooner had,
Past reason hated, as a swallow'd bait
On purpose laid to make the taker mad, –
Mad in pursuit, and in possession so;
Had, having, and in quest to have, extreme;
A bliss in proof; and prov'd, a very woe;
Before, a joy propos'd; behind, a dream.
    All this the world well knows; yet none knows well
    To shun the heaven that leads men to this hell.

147

My love is as a fever, longing still
For that which longer nurseth the disease,
Feeding on that which doth preserve the ill,
The uncertain sickly appetite to please.
My reason, the physician to my love,
Angry that his prescriptions are not kept,
Hath left me, and I desperate now approve
Desire is death, which physic did except.
Past cure I am now reason is past care,
And frantic mad with evermore unrest;
My thoughts and my discourse as madmen's are,
At random from the truth, vainly express'd:
    For I have sworn thee fair, and thought thee bright,
    Who art black as hell, as dark as night.

from Venus and Adonis

'Fondling,' she saith 'since I have hemm'd thee here
Within the circuit of this ivory pale,
I'll be a park, and thou shalt be my deer;
Feed where thou wilt, on mountain or in dale;
    Graze on my lips; and if those hills be dry,
    Stray lower, where the pleasant fountains lie.

'Within this limit is relief enough,
Sweet bottom-grass, and high delightful plain,
Round rising hillocks, brakes obscure and rough,
To shelter thee from tempest and from rain;
    Then be my deer, since I am such a park;
    No dog shall rouse thee, though a thousand bark.'

Venus and Adonis (229-240)

from Love's Labour's Lost

"But love, first learned in a lady's eyes"

But love, first learned in a lady's eyes,
Lives not alone immured in the brain,
But with the motion of all elements
Courses as swift as thought in every power,
And gives to every power a double power,
Above their functions and their offices.
It adds a precious seeing to the eye:
A lover's eyes will gaze an eagle blind.
A lover's ear will hear the lowest sound,
When the suspicious head of theft is stopp'd.
Love's feeling is more soft and sensible
Than are the tender horns of cockled snails;
Love's tongue proves dainty Bacchus gross in taste.
For valour, is not Love a Hercules,
Still climbing trees in the Hesperides?
Subtle as Sphinx; as sweet and musical
As bright Apollo's lute, strung with his hair.
And when Love speaks, the voice of all the gods
Make heaven drowsy with the harmony.
Never durst poet touch a pen to write
Until his ink were temp'red with love's sighs;
O, then his lines would ravish savage ears,
And plant in tyrants mild humility.
From women's eyes this doctrine I derive.
They sparkle still the right Promethean fire;
They are the books, the arts, the academes,
That show, contain, and nourish, all the world,
Else none at all in aught proves excellent.

Berowne. *Love's Labour's Lost*, 4.3.323-350

from Romeo and Juliet

"Gallop apace, you fiery-footed steeds"

Gallop apace, you fiery-footed steeds
Towards Phoebus' lodging; such a waggoner
As Phaethon would whip you to the west,
And bring in cloudy night immediately.
Spread thy close curtain, love-performing night,
That runaways' eyes may wink, and Romeo
Leap to these arms, untalk'd of and unseen.
Lovers can see to do their amorous rites
By their own beauties; or if love be blind,
It best agrees with night. Come, civil night,
Thou sober-suited matron, all in black,
And learn me how to lose a winning match,
Play'd for a pair of stainless maidenhoods;
Hood my unmann'd blood, bating in my cheeks,
With thy black mantle, till strange love, grown bold,
Think true love acted simple modesty.
Come, night; come, Romeo; come, thou day in night;
For thou wilt lie upon the wings of night
Whiter than new snow on a raven's back.
Come, gentle night, come, loving black-brow'd night,
Give me my Romeo; and, when he shall die,
Take him and cut him out in little stars,
And he will make the face of heaven so fine
That all the world will be in love with night,
And pay no worship to the garish sun.

Juliet. *Romeo and Juliet*, 3.1.1-25

THOMAS CAMPION
(1567-1620)

"My sweetest Lesbia"

My sweetest Lesbia, let us live and love;
And, though the sager sort our deeds reprove,
Let us not weigh them. Heaven's great lamps do dive
Into their west, and straight again revive.
But soon as once set is our little light,
Then must we sleep one ever-during night.

If all would lead their lives in love like me,
Then bloody swords and armour should not be;
No drum no trumpet peaceful sleeps should move,
Unless alarm came from the camp of Love.
But fools do live and waste their little light,
And seek with pain their ever-during night.

When timely death my life and fortune ends,
Let not my hearse be vexed with mourning friends,
But let all lovers, rich in triumph, come
And with sweet pastimes grace my happy tomb.
And, Lesbia, close up thou my little light,
And crown with love my ever-during night.

"What then is love but mourning?"

What then is love but mourning?
  What desire, but a self-burning?
Till she that hates doth love return,
Thus will I mourn, thus will I sing,
  Come away, come away, my darling.

Beauty is but a blooming,
  Youth in his glory entombing;
Time hath a wheel, which none can stay:
Then come away, while thus I sing,
  Come away, come away, my darling.

Summer in winter fadeth;
  Gloomy night heav'nly light shadeth:
Like to the morn are Venus flowers;
Such are her howers: then will I sing,
  Come away, come away, my darling.

"Hark, all you ladies that do weep"

Hark, all you ladies that do sleep,
   The fairy queen Prosperina
Bids you awake, and pity them that weep.
      You may do in the dark
        What the day doth forbid.
      Fear not the dogs that bark;
        Night will have all hid.

But if you let your lovers moan,
   The fairy queen Prosperina
Will send abroad her fairies every one,
      That shall pinch black and blue
        Your white hands and fair arms,
      That did no kindly rue
        Your paramours' harms.

In myrtle arbours on the downs,
   The fairy queen Prosperina,
This night by moonshine, leading merry rounds,
      Holds a watch with sweet love,
        Down the dale, up the hill;
      No complaints or groans may move
        Their holy vigil.

All you that will hold watch with Love,
   The fairy queen Prosperina
Will make you fairer than Dione's dove.
      Roses red, lilies white,
        And the clear damask hue,
      Shall on your cheeks alight.
        Love will adorn you.

All you that love or loved before,
   The fairy queen Prosperina
Bids you increase that loving humour more.
      they that have not yet fed
        On delight amorous,
      She vows that they shall ela
        Apes in Avernus.

BEN JONSON
(1573-1637)

To Celia

Come my Celia, let us prove,
While we may, the sports of love;
Time will not be ours, for ever:
He, at length, our good will sever.
Spend not then his gifts in vain.
Sunnes, that set, may rise again:
But if once we loose this light,
'Tis, with us, perpetual night.
Why should we defer our joys?
Fame, and rumour are but toys.
Cannot we delude the eyes
Of a few poor houshold spies?
Or his easier ears beguile,
So removed by our wile?
'Tis no sin, loves fruit to steale,
But the sweet theft to reveal:
To be taken, to be seen,
These have crimes accounted been.

JOHN DONNE

(1573-1631)

The Extasie

Where, like a pillow on a bed,
  A pregnant bank swelled up, to rest
The violet's reclining head,
  Sat we two, one another's best;

Our hands were firmly cemented
  With a false balm, which thence did spring,
Our eye-beams twisted, and did thread
  Our eyes, upon one double string;

So to' intergraft our hands, as yet
  Was all our means to make us one,
And pictures in our eyes to get
  Was all our propagation.

As 'twixt two equal armies, Fate
  Suspends uncertain victory,
Our souls, (which to advance their state,
  Were gone), hung 'twixt her, and me.

And whilst our souls negotiate there,
  We like sepulchral statues lay;
All day, the same our postures were,
  And we said nothing, all the day.

If any, so by love refined,
  That he soul's language understood,
And by good love were grown all mind,
  Within convenient distance stood,

He (though he knew not which soul spake
  Because both meant, both spake the same)
Might thence a new concoction take,
  And part far purer than he came.

* 61

This extasie doth unperplex
    (We said) and tell us what we love,
We see by this, it was not sex,
    We see, we saw not what did move:

But as all several souls contain
    Mixture of things, they know not what,
Love, these mixed souls doth mix again,
    And makes both one, each this and that.

A single violet transplant,
    The strength, the colour, and the size,
(All which before was poor, and scant,)
    Redoubles still, and multiplies.

When love, with one another so
    Interinanimates two souls,
That abler soul, which thence doth flow,
    Defects of loneliness controls.

We then, who are this new soul, know,
    Of what we are composed, and made,
For, th' atomies of which we grow,
    Are souls, whom no change can invade.

But O alas, so long, so far
    Our bodies why do we forbear?
They are ours, though they are not we, we are
    The intelligences, they the sphere.

We owe them thanks, because they thus,
    Did us, at first convey,
Yielded their forces, sense, to us,
    Nor are dross to us, but allay.

On man heaven's influences works not so,
    But that it first imprints the air,
So soul into the soul may flow,
    Though it to body first repair.

As our blood labours to beget
    Spirits, as like souls as it can,
Because such fingers need to knit
    That subtle knot, which makes us man:

So must pure lovers' souls descend
  T' affections, and to faculties,
Which sense may reach and apprehend,
  Else a great prince in prison lies.

To our bodies turn we then, that so
  Weak men on love revealed may look;
Love's mysteries in souls do grow,
  But yet the body is his book.

And if some lover, such as we,
  Have heard this dialogue of one,
Let him still mark us, he shall see
  Small change, when we' are to bodies gone.

from Elegy: To His Mistress Going to Bed

Licence my roving hands, and let them go
Before, behind, between, above, below.
O my America, my new found land,
My kingdom, safeliest when with one man manned,
My mine of precious stones, my empery,
How blessed am I in this discovering thee!
To enter in these bonds, is to be free;
Then where my hand is set, my seal shall be.
Full nakedness, all joys are due to thee.
As souls unbodied, bodies unclothed must be,
To taste whole joys.

Love's Alchemy

Some that have deeper digged love's mine than I,
Say, where his centric happiness doth lie:
     I have loved, and got, and told,
But should I love, get, tell, till I were old,
I should not find that hidden mystery;
     Oh, 'tis impostur all:
And as no chemic yet the elixir got,
     But glorifies his pregnant pot,
     If by the way to him befall
Some odoriferous thing, or medicinal,
  So, lovers dreams a rich and long delight,
  But get a winter-seeming summer's night.

Our ease, our thrift, our honour, and our day,
Shall we, for this vain bubble's shadow pay?
     Ends love in this, that my man,
Can be as happy as I can; if he can
Endure the short scorn of a bridegroom's play?
     That loving wretch that swears,
'Tis not the bodies marry, but her angelic finds,
     Would swear as justly, that he hears,
In that day's rude hoarse minstrelsy, the spheres.
Hope not for mind in women; at their best
  Sweetness and wit, they are but mummy, possessed.

The Bait

Come live with me, and by my love,
And we will some new pleasures prove
Of golden sands, and crystal brooks,
With silken lines, and silver hooks.

There will the river whispering run
Warmed by thy eyes, more than the sun.
And there the' enamoured fish will stay,
Begging themselves they may betray.

When thou wilt swim in that live bath,
Each fish, which every channel hath,
Will amorously to thee swim,
Gladder to catch thee, than thou him.

If thou, to be so seen, be'st loth,
By sun, or moon, thou darkenest both,
And if myself have leave to see,
I need not their light, having thee.

Lets others freeze with angling reeds,
And cut their legs, with shells and weeds,
Or treacherously poor fish beset,
With strangling snare, or windowy net:

Let coarse bold hands, from slimy nest
The bedded fish in banks out-wrest,
Or curious traitors, sleavesilk flies
Bewitch poor fishes' wandering eyes.

For thee, thou need'st no such deceit,
For thou thyself art thine own bait,
That fish, that is not catched thereby,
Alas, is wiser far than I.

Air and Angels

Twice or thrice had I loved thee,
Before I knew thy face or name;
So in a voice, so in a shapeless flame,
Angels affect us oft, and worshipped be;
  Still, when, to where thou wert, I came,
Some lovely glorious nothing I did see,
  But since my soul, whose child love is,
Takes limbs of flesh, and else could nothing do,
  More subtle than the parent is
Love must not be, but take a body too,
    And therefore what thou wert, and who
      I bid love ask, and now
That it assume thy body, I allow,
And fix itself in thy lip, eye, and brow.

Whilst thus to ballast love, I thought,
And so more steadily to have gone,
With waves which would sink admiration,
I saw, I had love's pinnace overfraught,
  Every thy hair for love to work upon
Is much too much, some fitter must be sought;
  For, nor in nothing, nor in things
Extreme, and scatt'rings bright, can love in here;
  Then as an angel, face and wings
Of air, not pure as it, yet pure doth wear,
  So thy love may be my love's sphere;
    Just such disparity
As is 'twixt air and angels' purity,
'Twixt women's love, and men's will ever be.

ROBERT HERRICK
(1591-1674)

To Phillis to Love, and Live With Him

Live, live with me, and thou shalt see
The pleasures I'll prepare for thee:
What sweets the Country can afford
Shall blesse thy Bed, and blesse thy Board.
The soft sweet Mosse shall be thy bed,
With crawling Woodbine over-spread:
By which the silver-shedding streames
Shall gently melt thee into dreames.
Thy clothing next, shall be a Gowne
Made of the Fleeces purest Downe.
The tongues of Kids shall be thy meate;
Their Milke thy drinke; and thou shalt eate
The Pastes of Filberts for thy bread
With Cream of Cowslip buttered:
Thy Feasting-Tables shall be Hills
With *Daisies* spread, and *Daffadils*;
Where thou shalt sit, and *Red-brest* by,
For meat, shall give thee melody.
I'll give thee Chaines and Carkanets
Of *Primroses* and *Violets*.
A Bag and Bottle thou shalt have;
That richly wrought, and This as brave;
So that as either shall expresse
The Wearer's no meane Shepheardesse.
At Sheering-times, and yearely Wakes,
When *Themilis* his pastime makes,
There thou shalt be; and be the wit,
Nay more, the Feast, and grace of it.
On holy-dayes, when Virgins meet
To dance the Heyes with nimble feet;
Thou shalt come forth, and then appeare
Then *Queen of Roses* for that yeere.
And having danc't ('bove all the best)
Carry the Garland from the rest.
In Wicker-baskets Maids shall bring
To thee, (my dearest Shepharling)

The blushing Apple, bashfull Peare,
And shame-fac't Plum, (all simp'ring there).
Walk in the Groves, and thou shalt find
The name of *Phillis* in the Rind
Of every straight, and smooth-skin tree;
Where kissing that, I'll twice kisse thee.
To thee a Sheep-hook I will send,
Be-pranckt with Ribbands, to this end,
This, this alluring Hook might be
Lesse for to catch a sheep, then me.
Thou shalt have Possets, Wassails fine,
Not made of Ale, but spiced Wine;
To make thy Maids and selfe free mirth,
All sitting neer the glitt'ring hearth.
Thou sha't have Ribbands, Roses, Rings,
Gloves, Garters, Stockings, Shooes, and Strings
Of winning Colours, that shall move
Others to Lust, but me to Love.
These (nay) and more, thine own shall be,
If thou wilt love, and live with me.

A Conjuration, to Electra

By those soft Tods of wool
With which the air is full:
By all those trinctures there,
That paint the hemisphere:
By dews and drizzling rain,
That swell the golden grain:
By all those sweets that he
I' the flow'ry nunnery:
By silent nights, and the
Three forms of Hecate:
By all aspects that bless
The sober sorceress,
While juice she strains, and pith
To make her philtres with:
By Time, that hastens on
Things to perfection:
And by your self, the best
Conjurement of the rest:
Of my Electra! be
In love with none, but me.

To Electra

I dare not ask a kisse;
  I dare not beg a smile;
Lest having that, or this,
  I might grow proud the while.

No, no, the utmost share
  Of my desire, shall be
Only to kisse that Aire,
  That lately kissed thee.

Upon Julia's Clothes

When as in silks my Julia goes,
Then, then (me thinks) how sweetly flowes
That liquefaction of her clothes.

Next, when I cast mine eyes and see
That brave Vibration each way free;
O how that glittering taketh me!

ANNE BRADSTREET
(1613?-1672)

To My Dear and Living Husband

If ever two were one, then surely we.
If ever man were loved by wife, then thee;
If ever wife was happy in a man,
Compare with me, ye women, if you can.
I prize thy love more than whole mines of gold
Or all the riches that the East doth hold.
My love is such that rivers cannot quench,
Nor ought but love from thee, give recompense.
Thy love is such I can no way repay,
The heavens reward thee manifold, I pray.
Then while we live, in love let's so persevere
That when we live no more, we may love ever.

HENRY VAUGHAN

(1621-1695)

To Amoret, Walking in a Starry Evening

If *Amoret*, that glorious eye,
    In the first birth of light,
      And death of night,
Had with those elder fires you spy
    Scattered so high
    Received form, and sight;

We might suspect in the vast Ring,
    Amidst these golden glories,
      And fiery stories;
Whether the Sun had been the King,
    And guide of Day,
    Or your brighter eye should sway;

But, *Amoret,* such is my fate,
    That if thy face a Star
      Had shined from far,
I am persuaded in that state
    'Twixt thee, and me,
    Of some predestined sympathy.

For sure such two conspiring minds,
    Which no accident, or sight,
      Did thus unite;
Whom no distance can confine,
    Start, or decline,
One, for another, were designed.

THOMAS TRAHERNE
(1636?-1674)

Love

O nectar! O delicious stream!
O ravishing and only pleasure! Where
        Shall such another theme
Inspire my tongue with joy or please mine ear!
        Abrigement of delights!
            And Queen of sights!
O mine of rarities! O Kingdom wide!
O more! O cause of all! O glorious Bride!
    O God! O Bride of God! O King!
    O soul and crown of everything!

    Did not I covet to behold
Some endless monarch, that did always live
        In palaces of gold,
Willing all kingdoms, realms, and crowns to give
        Unto my soul! Whose love
            A spring might prove
Of endless glories, honours, friendships, pleasures,
Joys, praises, beauties and celestial treasures!
    Lo, now I see there's such a King,
    The fountain-head of everything!

    Did my ambition ever dream
Of such a Lord, of such a love! Did I
        Expect so sweet a stream
As this at any time! Could any eye
        Believe it? Why all power
            Is used here;
Joys down from Heaven on my head do shower,
And Jove beyond the fiction doth appear
    Once more in golden rain to come
    To Danae's pleasing fruitful womb.

His Ganymede! His life! His joy!
Or He comes down to me, or takes me up
    That I might be His boy,
And fill, and taste, and give, and drink the cup.
    But those (tho' great) are all
      Too short and small,
Too weak and feeble pictures to express
The true mysterious depths of Blesseness.
    I am His image, and His friend,
    His son, bride, glory, temple, end.

APHRA BEHN
(1640-1689)

Song: The Willing Mistress

Amyntas led me to a grove
   Where all the trees did shade us;
The sun it self, though it had strove,
   It could not have betrayed us:
The place secured from human eyes,
   No other fear allows,
But when the winds that gently rise,
   Does kiss the yielding boughs.

Down there we sat upon the moss,
   And did begin to play
A thousand amorous tricks, to pass
   The heat of all the day.
A many kisses he did give;
   And I returned the same
Which made me willing to receive
   That which I dare not name.

His charming eyes no aid required
   To tell their soft'ning tale;
On her that was already fired
   'Twas easy to prevail.
He did but kiss and clasp me round,
   Whilst those his thoughts expressed:
And laid me gently on the ground;
   Ah who can guess the rest?

MEURSIUS

(18th century)

from *The Delights of Venus*

Then from the window he an ointment brought,
Which his too hasty passion had forgot.
His prick smelt sweet with what he rubb'd upon't,
And seem'd as fitting for my mouth as cunt.
As soon as this was done, he made me rise,
And place myself upon my hands and thighs.
My head down stooping on the bed did lie,
But my round buttocks lifted were on high,
Just like a cannon plac'd against the sky.
My bloody smock he then turn'd up behind,
As if to bugger me he had design'd:
Then with his sweet and slipp'ry prick drew near,
And vig'rously he charg'd me in the rear.
His prick, as soon as to my cunt apply'd,
Up to the hilt into my cunt did slide.
He fucked, and ask'd me if my cunt was sore?
Or his prick hurt me as it did before:
   I answer'd, No, my dear; no, do not cease;
But oh! do thus as long as ever you please.
This stroke did fully answer our intent
For at one moment both together spent
Just as we fuck'd, I cry'd, I faint, I die,
And fell down in a blissful ecstasy...

PERCY BYSSHE SHELLEY

(1792-1822)

Love's Philosophy

I

The fountains mingle with the river
    And the rivers with the Ocean,
The winds of heaven mix for ever
    With a sweet emotion;
Nothing in the world is single;
    All things by a law divine
In one spirit meet and mingle.
    Why not I with thine? –

II

See the mountains kiss high Heaven
    And the waves clasp one another;
No sister-flower would be forgiven
    If it disdained its brother;
And the sunlight clasps the earth
    And the moonbeams kiss the sea:
What is all this sweet work worth
    If thou kiss not me?

from Epipsychidion

Meanwhile
We two will rise, and sit, and walk together,
Under the roof of blue Ionian weather,
And wander in the meadows, or ascend
The mossy mountains, where the blue heavens bend
With lightest winds, to touch their paramour;
Or linger, where the pebble-paven shore,
Under the quick, faint kisses of the sea
Possessing and possessed by all that is
Within that calm circumference of bliss,
And by each other, till to love and live
Be one: – or, at the noontide hour, arrive
Where some old cavern hoar seems yet to keep
The moonlight of the expired night asleep,
Through which the awakened day can never peep;
A Veil for our seclusion, close as night's,
Where secure sleep may kill thine innocent lights;
Sleep, the fresh dew of languid love, the rain
Whose drops quench kisses till they burn again.
And we will talk, until thought's melody
Become too sweet for utterance, and it die
In words, to live again in looks, which dart
With thrilling tone into the voiceless heart,
Harmonizing silence without a sound.
Our breathing shall intermix, our bosoms bound,
And our veins beat together; and our lips
With other eloquence than words, eclipse
The soul that burns between them, and the wells
Which boil under our being's inmost cells,
The fountains of our deepest life, shall be
Confused in Passion's golden purity,
As mountain-springs under the morning sun.
We shall become the same, we shall be one
Spirit within two frames, oh! wherefore two?
One passion in twin-hearts, which grows and grew,
Till like two meteors of expanding flame.
Those spheres instinct with it become the same,
Touch, mingle, are transfigured; ever still
Burning, yet ever inconsumable:
In one another's substance finding food,
Like flames too pure and light and unimbued

* *80*

To nourish their bright lives with baser prey,
Which point to heaven and cannot pass away:
One hope within two wills, one will beneath
Two overshadowing minds, one life, one death,
One heaven, one Hell, one immortality,
And one annihilation. Woe is me!
The wingèd words on which my soul would pierce
Into the height of Love's rare Universe,
Are chains of lead around its flight of fire –
I pant, I sink, I tremble, I expire!

from Prometheus Unbound

Panthea:…I saw not, heard not, moved not, only felt
His presence flow and mingle through my blood
Till it became his life, and his grew mine,
And I was thus absorbed, until it passed,
And like the vapours when the sun sinks down,
Gathering again in drops upon the pines,
And tremulous as they, in the deep night
My being was condensed…
I always knew what I desired before,
Nor ever found delight to wish in vain.
But now I cannot tell thee what I seek;
Even to desire; it is thy sport, false sister;
Thou hast discovered some enchantment old,
Whose spells have stolen my spirit as I slept
And mingled it with thine: for when just now
We kissed, I felt within thy parted lips
The sweet air that sustained me, and the warmth
Of the life-blood, for loss of which I faint,
Quivered between our intertwining arms.

JOHN KEATS
(1795-1821)

from Isabella

IX

'Love! thou art leading me from wintry cold,
    Lady! thou leadest me to summer clime,
And I must taste the blossoms that unfold
    In its ripe warmth this gracious morning time.'
So said, his erstwhile timid lips grew bold,
    And poesied with hers in dewy rhyme:
Great bliss was with them, and great happiness
Grew, like a lusty flower in June's caress.

X

Parting they seem'd to tread upon the air,
    Twin roses by the zephyr blown apart
Only to meet again more close, and share
    The inward fragrance of each other's heart.
She, to her chamber gone, a ditty fair
    Sang, of delicious love and honey'd dart;
He with light steps went up a western hill,
And bade the sun farewell, and joy'd his fill.

from Lines to Fanny

O, for some sunny spell
To dissipate the shadows of this hell!
Say they are gone, - with the new dawning light
Steps forth my lady bright!
O, let me once more rest
My soul upon that dazzling breast!
Let once again these aching arms be plac'd,
The tender gaolets of thy waist!
And let me feel that warm breath here and there
To spread a rapture in my very hair, -
O, the sweetness of the pain!
Give me those lips again!
Enough! Enough! it is enough for me
To dream of thee!

La Belle Dame Sans Merci

I

O what can ail thee, knight-at-arms,
 Alone and palely loitering?
The sedge is wither'd from the lake,
 And no birds sing.

II

O what can ail thee, knight-at-arms,
 So haggard and so woe-begone?
The squirrel's granary is full,
 And the harvest's done.

III

I see a lily on thy brow
 With anguish moist and fever dew;
And on thy cheek a fading rose
 Fast withereth too.

IV

I met a lady in the meads,
 Full beautiful – a faery's child,
Her hair was long, her foot was light,
 And her eyes were wild.
V

I made a garland for her head,
 And bracelets too, and fragrant zone;
She look'd at me as she did love
 And made sweet moan.

VI

I set her on my pacing steed,
 And nothing else saw all day long,
For sideways would she lean, and sing
 A faery's song.

VII

She found me roots of relish sweet,
    And honey wild, and manna dew;
And sure in language strange she said –
    'I love thee true!'

VIII

She took me to her elfin grot,
    And there she gazed and sigh'd full sore,
And there I shut her wild wild eyes
    With kisses four.

IX

And there she lulled me asleep,
    And there I dream'd – ah! woe betide!\
The latest dream I ever dream'd
    On the cold hill side.

X

I saw pale kings and princes too,
    Pale warriors, death-pale were they all;
Who cried – 'La Belle Dame Sans Merci
    Hath thee in thrall!'

XI

I saw their starv'd lips in the gloam,
    With horrid warning gaped wide,
And I awoke, and found me here,
    On the cold hillside.

XII

And this is why I sojourn here,
    Alone and palely loitering,
Though the sedge is wither'd from the lake,
    And no birds sing.

MARY WOLLSTONECRAFT SHELLEY
(1797-1851)

Stanzas

Oh, come to me in dreams, my love!
  I will not ask a dearer bliss;
Come with the starry beams, my love,
  And press mine eyelids with thy kiss.

'Twas thus, as ancient fables tell,
  Love visited a Grecian maid,
Till she disturbed the sacred spell,
  And woke to find her hopes betrayed.

But gentle sleep shall veil my sight,
  And Psyche's lamp shall darkling be.
When, in the visions of the night,
  Thou dost renew thy vows to me.

Then come to me in dreams, my love,
  I will not ask a dearer bliss:
Come with the starry beams, my love,
  And press mine eyelids with thy kiss.

JOHN CLARE
(1793-1864)

To Mary

It is the evening hour,
　　How silent all doth lie:
The hornèd moon she shows her face
　　In the river with the sky.
Prest by the path on which we pass,
The flaggy lake lies still as glass.

Spirit of her I love,
　　Whispering to me
Stores of sweet visions as I rove,
　　Here stop, and crop with me
Sweet flowers that in the still hour grew -
We'll take them home, nor shake off the bright dew.

Mary, or sweet spirit of thee,
　　As the bright sun shines tomorrow
Thy dark eyes these flowers shall seem
　　Gathered by me in sorrow,
In the still hour when my mind was free
To walk alone - yet wish I walked with thee.

ELIZABETH BARRET BROWNING
(1806-1861)

from Sonnets from the Portuguese

Say over again, and yet once over again,
That thou dost love me. Though the word repeated
Should seem 'a cuckoo-song,' as thou dost treat it.
Remember, never to the hill or plain,
Valley and wood, without her cuckoo-strain
Comes the fresh Spring in all her green completed.
Belovèd, I, amid the darkness greeted
By a doubtful spirit-voice, in that doubt's pain
Cry... 'Speak once more... thou lovest!' Who can fear
Too many stars, though each in heaven shall roll, –
Too many flowers, though each shall crown the year?
Say thou love me, love me, love me – toll
The silver iterance! – only minding, Dear,
To love me also in silence with thy soul.

When our two souls stand up erect and strong,
Face to face, silent, drawing nigh and nigher,
Until the lengthening wings break into fire
At either curvèd point, – what bitter wrong
Can the earth do to us, that we should not long
Be here contented? Think. In mounting higher,
The angels would press us on and aspire
To drop some golden orb of perfect song
Into our deep, dear silence. Let us stay
Rather on earth, Belovèd – where the unfit
Contrarious moods of men recoil away
And isolate pure spirits, and permit
A place to stand and love in for a day,
With darkness and the death-hour rounding it.

EMILY BRONTE
(1818-1848)

"O wander not so far away!"

O wander not so far away!
O love, forgive this selfish tear.
It may be sad for thee to stay
But how can I live lonely here?

The still May morn is warm and bright,
Young flowers look fresh and grass is green,
And in the haze of glorious light
Our long low hills are scarcely seen.

The woods - even now their small leaves hides
The blackbird and the stockdove well
And high in heaven so blue and wide
A thousand strains of music swell.

He looks on all with eyes that speak
So deep, so drear a woe to me!
There is a faint red on his cheek
Not like the bloom I used to see.

Call Death - yes, Death, he is thine own!
The grave must close those limbs around
And hush, for ever hush the tone
I lived above all earthly sound.

Well, pass away with the other flowers,
Too dark for them, too dark for thee
Are the hours to come, the joyless hours
That Time is treasuring up for me -

If thou hast sinned in this world of care
'Twas but the dust of thy drear abode -
Thy soul was pure when it entered here
And pure it will go again to God!

Stanzas

I'll not weep that thou art going to leave me,
There's nothing lovely here;
And doubly will the dark world grieve me,
While thy heart suffers there.

I'll not weep, because the summer's glory
Must always end in gloom;
And, follow out the happiest story –
It closes with a tomb!

And I am weary of the anguish
Increasing winters bear;
Weary to watch the spirit languish
Through years of dead despair.

So, if a tear, when thou art dying,
Should haply fall from me,
It is but that my soul is sighing,
To go and rest with thee.

CHRISTINA ROSSETTI
(1830-1894)

Echo

Come to me in the silence of the night;
   Come in the speaking silence of a dream;
Come with soft rounded cheeks and eyes as bright
    As sunlight on a stream;
      Come back in tears,
O memory, hope, love of finished years.

O dream how sweet, too sweet, too bitter sweet,
   Whose wakening should have been in paradise,
Where souls brimfull of love abide and meet,
    Where thirsting longing eyes
      Watch the slow door
That opening, letting in, lets out no more.

Yet come to me in dreams, that I may live
   My very life again though cold in death:
Come back to me in dreams, that I may give
    Pulse for pulse, breath for breath:
      Speak low, lean low,
As long ago, my love, how long ago.

EMILY DICKINSON
(1830-1886)

"Wild Night - Wild Nights!"

Wild Nights! - Wild Nights!
Were I with thee
Wild Nights should be
Our luxury!

Futile - the Winds -
To a Heart in port -
Done with the Compass -
Done with the Chart!

Rowing in Eden -
Ah, the sea!
Might I but moor - Tonight -
In Thee!

"To wait an Hour - is long"

To wait an Hour - is long -
If Love be just beyond -
To wait Eternity - is short -
If love reward the end -

"Unable are the Loved to die"

Unable are the Loved to die
For Love is Immortality,
Nay, it is Deity –

Unable they that love – to die
For Love reforms Vitality
Into Divinity.

THOMAS HARDY
(1840-1928)

Her Haunting Ground

Can it be so? It must be so,
That visions have not ceased to be
In this the chiefest sanctuary
Of her whose form we used to know.
– Nay, but her dust is far away,
And 'where her dust is, shapes her shade,
If spirit clings to flesh,,' they say:
Yet here her life-parts most were played!

Her voice explored this atmosphere,
Her foot impressed this turf around,
Her shadow swept this slope and mound,
Her fingers fondled blossoms here;
And so, I ask, why, why should she
Haunt elsewhere, by a slighted tomb,
When here she flourished sorrow-free,
And, save for others, knew no gloom?

Thoughts of Phena

At news of her death

Not a line of her writing have I,
    Not a thread of her hair,
No mark of her late time as dame in her dwelling, whereby
    I may picture her there;
  And in vain do I urge my unsight
    To conceive my lost prize
At her close, whom I knew when her dreams were
Upbrimming with light,
  And with laughter her eyes.

What scene spread around her last days,
    Sad, shining, or dim?
Did her gifts and compassions enray and enarch her sweet ways
    With an aureate nimb?
  Or did life-light decline from her years,
    And mischances control
Her full day-star; unease, or regret, or forebodings, or fears
    Disennoble her soul?

Thus I do but the phantom retain
    Of the maiden of yore
As my relic; yet haply the best of her – fined in my brain
    It may be the more
  That no line of her writing have I,
    Nor a thread of her hair,
No mark of her late time as dame in her dwelling, whereby
    I may picture her there.

Growth in May

I enter a daisy-and-buttercup land,
    And thence thread a jungle of grass:
Hurdles and stiles scarce visible stand
    Above the lush stems as I pass.

Hedges peer over, and try to be seen,
    And seem to reveal a dim sense
That amid such ambitious and elbow-high green
    They made a mean show as a fence.

Elsewhere the mead is possessed of neats,
    That range not greatly above
The rich rank thicket which brushes their teats,
    And *her* gown, as she waits for her Love.

That Kiss in the Dark

     Recall it you? –
     Say you do! –
When you went out into the night,
In an impatience that would not wait,
From that lone house in the woodland spot,
And when I, thinking you had gone
For ever and ever from my sight,
Came after, printing a kiss upon
     Black air
     In my despair,
And my two lips lit on your cheek
As you leant silent against a gate,
Making my woman's face flush hot
At what I had done in the dark, unaware
You lingered for me but would not speak:
Yes, kissed you, thinking you were not there!
     Recall it you? –
     Say you do!

The Recalcitrants

Let us off and search, and find a place
Where yours and mine can be natural lives,
Where no one comes who Dissects and dives
And proclaims that ours is a curious case,
Which its touch of romance can scarcely grace.

You would think it strange at first, but then
Everything has been strange in its time.
When some one said on a day of the prime
He would bow to no brazen god again
He doubtless dazed the mass of men.

None will see in us a pair whose claims
To righteous judgment we care not making;
Who have doubted if breath he worth the taking,
And have no respect for the current fames
Whence the savour has flown while abide the names.

We have found us already shunned, disdained,
And for re-acceptance have not once striven;
Whatever offence our course has given
The brunt thereof we have long sustained.
Well, let us away, scorned, unexplained.

AMY LOWELL
(1874-1925)

Carrefour

O you,
Who came upon me once
Stretched under apple-trees just after bathing,
Why did you not strangle me before speaking
Rather than fill me with the wild white honey of your words
And then leave me to the mercy
Of the forest bees?

The Taxi

When I go away from you
The world beats dead
Like a slackened drum.
I call out for you against the jutted stars
And shout into the ridges of the wind.
Streets coming fast,
One after the other,
Wedge you away from me,
And the lamps of the city prick my eyes
So that I can no longer see your face.
Why should I leave you,
To wound myself upon the sharp edges of the night?

D.H. LAWRENCE
(1885-1930)

Leda

Come not with kisses
not with caresses
of hands and lips and murmurings;
come with a hiss of wings
and sea-touch tip of a beak
and treading of wet-webbed, wave-working feet
into the marsh-soft belly.

Lightning

I felt the lurch and halt of her heart
      Next my breast, where my own heart was beating;
And I laughed to feel it plunge and bound,
And strange in my blood-swept ears was the sound
      Of the words I kept repeating,
Repeating with tightened arms, and the hot blood's blindfold
                                     art.

Her breath flew warm against my neck,
      Warm as a flame in the close night air;
And the sense of her clinging flesh was sweet
Where her arms and my neck's blood-surge could meet.
      Holding her thus, did I care
That the black night hid her from me, blotted out every speck?

I leaned me forward to find her lips,
      And claim her utterly in a kiss,
When the lightning flew across her face,
And I saw her for the flaring space
      Of a second, afraid of the clips
Of my arms, inert with dread, wilted in fear of my kiss.

A moment, like a wavering spark,
      Her face lay there before my breast,
Pale lovelost in a snow of fear,
And guarded by a glittering tear,
      And lips apart with dumb cries;
A moment, and she was taken again in the merciful dark.

I heard the thunder, and felt the rain,
      And my arms fell loose, and I was dumb.
Almost I hated her, she was so good,
Hated myself, and the place, and my blood,
      Which burned with rage, as I bade her come
Home, away home, ere the lightning floated forth again.

GALLERY OF POETS

Sir Thomas Wyatt, by Hans Holbein, 1535-37

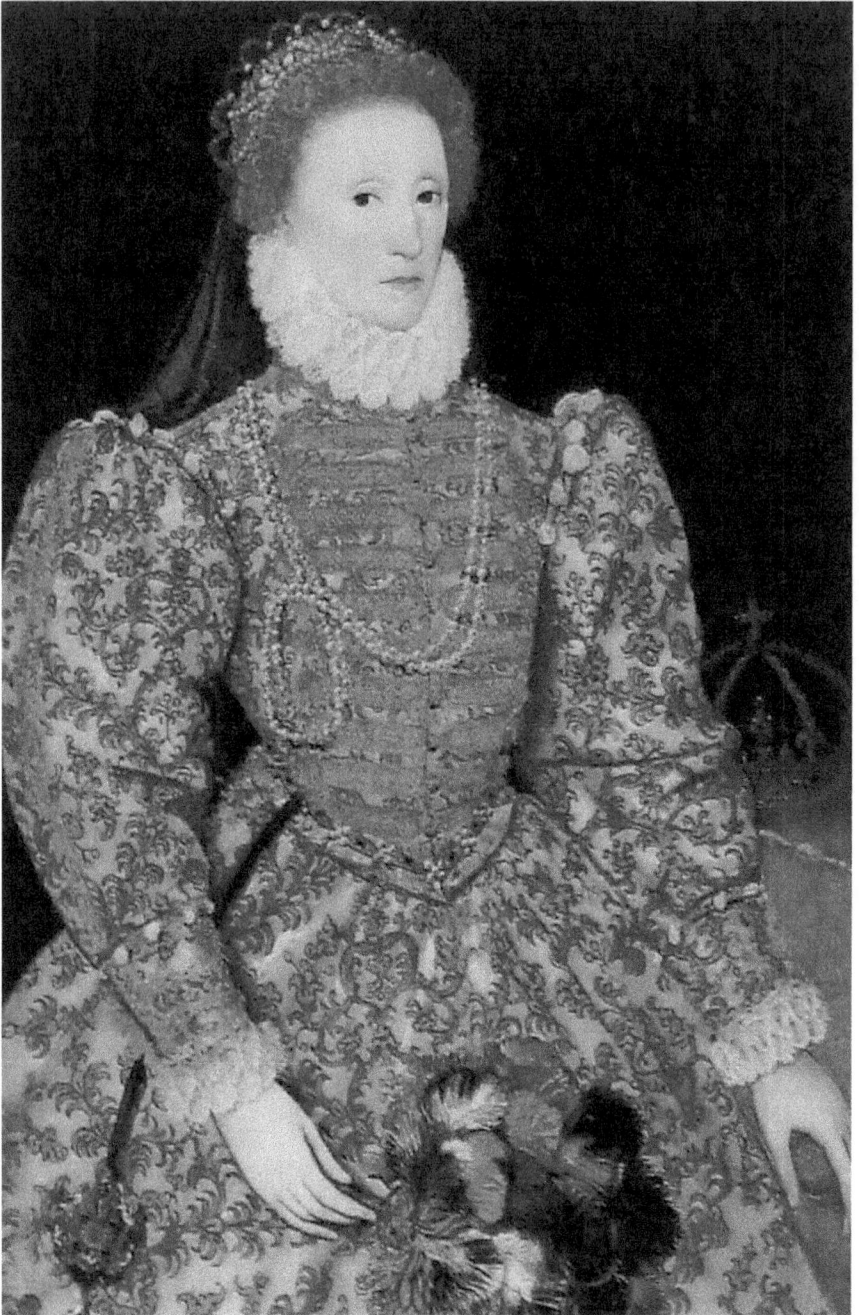

Elizabeth I, anonymous artist, 1575,
National Portrait Gallery, London

Samuel Daniel

Henry Constable

Michael Drayton

Christopher Marlowe, possibly, 1585

William Shakespeare

Thomas Campion, National Portrait Gallery, London

John Donne

Robert Herrick

Henry Vaughan

Percy Bysshe Shelley

John Keats

John Clare, by William Hilton, 1820, National Portrait Gallery, London

Elizabeth Barrett Browning, by Macaire Havre,1859.

The Brontë sisters, by their brother Bramwell, c. 1834

Emily Dickinson

Thomas Hardy

Amy Lowell

D.H. Lawrence

A NOTE ON LOVE POETRY

No book of love poetry would be complete without the master of the sonnet, Francesco Petrarch. As this is a book of love poems written originally in English, we cannot include Petrarch. A pity, because half the book could be taken up by selections from his magnificent *Canzoniere*. Petrarch's influence, however, can be felt throughout the history of English poetry. You find Petrarch most obviously in Thomas Wyatt, Shakespeare, John Donne, and the Elizabethan sonneteers: Samuel Daniel, Philip Sidney, Michael Drayton and Edmund Spenser. One could write a volume or two on Petrarch's influence on the Renaissance poets of Britain. You see Petrarch in those conceits and oppositions, for instance, where Wyatt speaks of burning and freezing with love. In his *Delia*, Samuel Daniel laments that he is not as great a poet as Petrarch: he loves just as much, even if he can't describe his fervour in the same fluid, luminous rhymes as the master Italian poet:

> Though thou, a Laura, hast no Petrarch found,
>   In base attire yet clearly beauty shines.
> And I, though born within a colder clime,
>   Do feel mine inward heat as great, I know it;
> He never had more faith, although more rhyme;
> I love as well, though he could better show it.

British poets could not, perhaps, show their love as eloquently as Petrarch in his *Rime Sparse*. The great love poem sequence, Shakespeare's *Sonnets*, comes closest to the grandeur and cleverness of Petrarch's *Rime*. In Shakespeare, introspection and self-analysis is as rigorous as in Petrarch, but Shakespeare's bitterness and sense of irony is more deeply ingrained than Petrarch's, and Shakespeare's *Sonnets* come late in the development of the sonnet genre. They are decadent, late efforts of an already (by the 1590s) old-fashioned poetic form. Yet Shakespeare manages to infuse the genre with an extraordinary power and magic. The *Sonnets*, indeed, contain some of the most marvellous of any (English) poetry. The *Sonnets* have a poetic authority that is hard to contest. Who can ignore the magnificence of these opening lines, for instance:

Shall I compare thee to a summer's day? (18.1)
Full many a glorious morning have I seen
Flatter the mountain tops with sovereign eye,
Kissing with golden face the meadows green,
Gilding pale streams with heavenly alchemy (33.1-4)
Let me confess that we two must be twain
Although our undivided loves are one (36.1-2)
Take all my loves, my love, yea, take them all (40.1)
Sweet love, renew thy force; be it not said (56.1)
Being your slave, what should I do but tend
Upon the hours and times of your desire? (57.1-2)
How like a winter hath my absence been
From thee, the pleasure of the fleeting year! (97.1-2)
To me, fair friend, you can never be old (104.1)
Let me not to the marriage of true minds
Admit impediments: love is not love
Which alters when it alteration finds,
Or bends with the remover to remove. (116.1-4)
The expense of spirit in a waste of shame
Is lust in action; and till action, lust
Is perjur'd, murderous, bloody, full of blame,
Savage, extreme, rude, cruel, not to trust (129.1-4)
My mistress' eyes are nothing like the sun (130.1)
My love is as a fever, longing still (147.1)

Like bells, these lines cut through, even after centuries of quotation and discussion. Nothing, it seems, has lessened the Bard's ability to create word magic. The sonnet, and especially the sonnet of love, became central to the

British poetic tradition between 1550 and 1650. Michael Spiller writes:

> With the exception of the Augustan poets in Britain, there have been few
> major poets who have not attempted sonnets... The existence of
> hundreds of thousands of sonnets in all the vernaculars of western
> Europe proves that, for 750 years at least, the sonnet has been
> challenging and satisfying the poetic imagination. The sonnet is probably
> the longest-lived of all poetic forms, and certainly the longest-lived of all
> *prescribed forms.*[1]

Michael Spiller goes on to discuss the British contribution to the sonnet
'vogue' or tradition:

> Alongside Torquato Tasso's 1,000 sonnets, the seven hundred or so
> sonnets of Ronsard, and the capacity of quite minor French and Italian
> writers to produce five or six hundred sonnets, the British contribution
> may even seem slender; yet it was concentrated, distinctive, and engaged
> the minds of the best writers of the age: Sidney, Spenser, and
> Shakespeare, Donne, Herbert and Milton... (ib., 83)

Sir Philip Sidney noted the self-deceit and self-manufacture of love
poetry, when he wrote in a sonnet in *Astrophil and Stella*:

> It is most true what we call Cupid's dart
> An image in which for ourselves we carve...

Love and love poetry is indeed something humans carve for themselves.
After all, this heterosexual, bourgeois, romantic love is not for the stars, the
grass, the animals, but only for humans.

The Renaissance love poem was as much artifice as emotion; perhaps the
ratio was more like 10% love and 90% art. Few of the Elizabethan love
poets, for instance, were actually in love with the people they were
writing about in their polished verses, as Michael Spiller notes:

> Why should a number of sonneteers have written love-poetry to women
> with whom they were not in love? Or to quite nonexistent women? Why
> should Robert Sidney have written a Petrarchan sequence of passionate
> complaint and melancholy while very happily and romantically married
> to his wife, Barbara Gamage? And why are so many sonnets translations

1 Michael R.G. Spiller: *The Development of the Sonnet: An Introduction*,
Routledge 1992, 1-2

or adaptions of other writers' work? One or two writers did indeed write their sonnets to women with whom they were fully and feasibly in love – Edmund Spenser, for example, and Drummond of Hawthorndem (probably)... (ib., 125)

Sir Philip Sidney also, in a first line of a sonnet from *Astrophil and Stella*, described precisely the origin of love poetry in emotional loss and sexual lack: 'O absent presence *Stella* is not here... (106) This is precisely where all the pain of love stems from, this Lacanian lack, which produces desire. The love poet is out of love, so s/he writes of love, wanting to be back in love. It's a simple equation, explaining also the emphasis in patriarchal poetry on love and death, on the connections between sex and pain. For, simply, to be out of love is to be not as alive as in love. So the out-of-love state is likened to death, the death-in-life, as some poets call it. The goal is not so much the beloved as love. For love poets are 'in love with love', to use St Bernard's terms, so apposite here. The love poem, then, arises from the lack, it fills the space between the lover and the loved. It becomes the æstheticization of love, love refined and distilled. As Michael Spiller writes:

> Desire...is the sense of an absence, or, more, exactly, a need to abolish an absence. It was Petrarch's extraordinary achievement to find in the sonnet a space where the movement between the desiring /I/ and its goal could be rhetorically mapped, by various linguistic devices that became the currency of poetic Europe. Thereafter, however desire might specifically be focused, the sonnet could express it, and Petrarchan love becomes a master analogy for all desire... (ib., 125)

Love poetry is founded on absence. The love poem becomes the stand-in for the presence of the beloved. Or as Emily Dickinson put it: 'So we must meet apart'. Love poetry luxuriates in the ambiguities and conflicts of love: it arises out of the very paradoxes that make love such a piquant topic for the artist. Emily Dickinson wrote of this erotic paradox in her poem "I cannot live with You", which, with its strange capitalizations and punctuation, and the Dickinson dash breaking up (or aiding) the flow of emotion, is ambiguous about the ambiguity of love, whether secular or sacred, erotic or Christian:

So we must meet apart
You there - I here -
With just the Door ajar
That Oceans are - and Prayer -

Emily Dickinson's poems included here, "Wild Nights - Wild Nights!", seems to be a more straight forward evocation of lust and erotic luxury. But, as Jan Montefiore comments, the poem

> evokes a discharge of energy sensed as forbidden excess, but it is entirely ambiguous whether the luxury is the storm of desire or the promise of shelter from it.[2]

Love poems mark an intersection between language and experience, between desire and gratification, between reality and dream. Many love poems are formed within a space of tension, a tension created by the poet and her/his desire. In this short, two stanza poem by Mary Coleridge (1861-1907), we find an evocation of the impossibility of love, the never-to-be-ness of love:

The clouds had made a crimson crown
About the mountains high.
The stormy sun was going down
In a stormy sky.

Why did you let your eyes so rest on me,
And hold your breath between?
In all the ages this can never be
As if it had not been.

Queen Elizabeth I also wrote love lyrics in the traditional, courtly manner. In her lovely poem 'On Monsieur's Departure', she describes the paradoxical nature of love, which encourages desire even while forbidding it. 'I love and yet am forced to seem to hate' writes Queen Elizabeth, acknowledging the social pressure that desire brings. To demonstrate the paradoxes of love, she employs the traditional poetic formula of the Renaissance, the Petrarchan conceit: 'I am and am not, I freeze and yet am burned'. The final stanza runs thus:

---

2 *Feminism and Poetry: Language, Experience, Identity in Women's Writing,* Jan Montefiore, Pandora, 1994, 168.

Some gentler passion slide into my mind,
For I am soft and made of melting snow;
Or be more cruel, love, and so be kind.
Let me float or sink, be high or low.
      Or let me live with some more sweet content,
      Or die and so forget what love e'er meant.

Beauties, Beasts, and Enchantment

CLASSIC FRENCH FAIRY TALES

Translated and with an Introduction
by Jack Zipes

A collection of 36 classic French fairy tales translated by renowned writer Jack Zipes.
Cinderella, Beauty and the Beast, Sleeping Beauty and *Little Red Riding Hood* are among the
classic fairy tales in this amazing book.
Includes illustrations from fairy tale collections.
Jack Zipes has written and published widely on fairy tales.

'Terrific... a succulent array of 17th and 18th century 'salon' fairy tales'
- *The New York Times Book Review*

'These tales are adventurous, thrilling in a way fairy tales are meant to be... The translation
from the French is modern, happily free of archaic and hyperbolic language... a fine and
sophisticated collection' - *New York Tribune*

'Enjoyable to read... a unique collection of French regional folklore' - *Library Journal*

'Charming stories accompanied by attractive pen-and-ink drawings' - *Chattanooga Times*

Introduction and illustrations   612pp.   ISBN 9781861712510 Pbk   ISBN 9781861713193 Hbk

Life, Life
Selected Poems

Arseny Tarkovsky

translated and edited by Virginia Rounding

Arseny Tarkovsky is the neglected Russian poet, father of the acclaimed film director Andrei Tarkovsky. This new book gathers together many of Tarkovsky's most lyrical and heartfelt poems, in Rounding's clear, new translations. Many of Tarkovsky's poems appeared in his son's films, such as *Mirror, Stalker, Nostalghia and The Sacrifice*. There is an introduction by Rounding, and a bibliography of both Arseny and Andrei Tarkovsky.

Bibliography and notes 124pp 3rd ed   ISBN 9781861712660 Hbk ISBN 9781861711144

In the Dim Void

Samuel Beckett's Late Trilogy:
Company, Ill Seen, Ill Said and *Worstward Ho*

by Gregory Johns

This book discusses the luminous beauty and dense, rigorous poetry of Samuel Beckett's late works, *Company, Ill Seen, Ill Said* and *Worstward Ho*. Gregory Johns looks back over Beckett's long writing career, charting the development from the *Molloy-Malone Dies-Unnamable* trilogy through the 'fizzles' of the 1960s to the elegiac lyricism of the *Company* series. Johns compares the trilogy with late plays such as *Ghosts, Footfalls* and *Rockaby*.

Bibliography, notes. Illustrated. 120pp
ISBN 9781861712974 Pbk and ISBN 9781861712608 Hbk
9781861713407 E-book

MAURICE SENDAK

& the art of children's book illustration

Maurice Sendak is the widely acclaimed American children's book author and illustrator. This critical study focuses on his famous trilogy, *Where the Wild Things Are*, *In the Night Kitchen* and *Outside Over There*, as well as the early works and Sendak's superb depictions of the Grimm Brothers' fairy tales in *The Juniper Tree*. L.M. Poole begins with a chapter on children's book illustration, in particular the treatment of fairy tales. Sendak's work is situated within the history of children's book illustration, and he is compared with many contemporary authors.

Fully illustrated. The book has been revised and updated for this edition.
ISBN 9781861714282 Pbk   ISBN 9781861713469 Hbk

CRESCENT MOON PUBLISHING

web: www.crmoon.com e-mail: cresmopub@yahoo.co.uk

ARTS, PAINTING, SCULPTURE

The Art of Andy Goldsworthy
Andy Goldsworthy: Touching Nature
Andy Goldsworthy in Close-Up
Andy Goldsworthy: Pocket Guide
Andy Goldsworthy In America
Land Art: A Complete Guide
The Art of Richard Long
Richard Long: Pocket Guide
Land Art In the UK
Land Art in Close-Up
Land Art In the U.S.A.
Land Art: Pocket Guide
Installation Art in Close-Up
Minimal Art and Artists In the 1960s and After
Colourfield Painting
Land Art DVD, TV documentary
Andy Goldsworthy DVD, TV documentary
The Erotic Object: Sexuality in Sculpture From Prehistory to the Present Day
Sex in Art: Pornography and Pleasure in Painting and Sculpture
Postwar Art
Sacred Gardens: The Garden in Myth, Religion and Art
Glorification: Religious Abstraction in Renaissance and 20th Century Art
Early Netherlandish Painting
Leonardo da Vinci
Piero della Francesca
Giovanni Bellini
Fra Angelico: Art and Religion in the Renaissance
Mark Rothko: The Art of Transcendence
Frank Stella: American Abstract Artist
Jasper Johns
Brice Marden
Alison Wilding: The Embrace of Sculpture
Vincent van Gogh: Visionary Landscapes
Eric Gill: Nuptials of God
Constantin Brancusi: Sculpting the Essence of Things
Max Beckmann
Caravaggio
Gustave Moreau
Egon Schiele: Sex and Death In Purple Stockings
Delizioso Fotografico Fervore: Works In Process 1
Sacro Cuore: Works In Process 2
The Light Eternal: J.M.W. Turner
The Madonna Glorified: Karen Arthurs

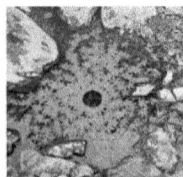

LITERATURE

J.R.R. Tolkien: The Books, The Films, The Whole Cultural Phenomenon
J.R.R. Tolkien: Pocket Guide
Tolkien's Heroic Quest
The *Earthsea* Books of Ursula Le Guin
Beauties, Beasts and Enchantment: Classic French Fairy Tales
German Popular Stories by the Brothers Grimm
Philip Pullman and *His Dark Materials*
Sexing Hardy: Thomas Hardy and Feminism
Thomas Hardy's *Tess of the d'Urbervilles*
Thomas Hardy's *Jude the Obscure*
Thomas Hardy: The Tragic Novels
Love and Tragedy: Thomas Hardy
The Poetry of Landscape in Hardy
Wessex Revisited: Thomas Hardy and John Cowper Powys
Wolfgang Iser: Essays and Interviews
Petrarch, Dante and the Troubadours
Maurice Sendak and the Art of Children's Book Illustration
Andrea Dworkin
Cixous, Irigaray, Kristeva: The *Jouissance* of French Feminism
Julia Kristeva: Art, Love, Melancholy, Philosophy, Semiotics and Psychoanalysis
Hélène Cixous I Love You: The *Jouissance* of Writing
Luce Irigaray: Lips, Kissing, and the Politics of Sexual Difference
Peter Redgrove: Here Comes the Flood
Peter Redgrove: Sex-Magic-Poetry-Cornwall
Lawrence Durrell: Between Love and Death, East and West
Love, Culture & Poetry: Lawrence Durrell
Cavafy: Anatomy of a Soul
German Romantic Poetry: Goethe, Novalis, Heine, Hölderlin
Feminism and Shakespeare
Shakespeare: Love, Poetry & Magic
The Passion of D.H. Lawrence
D.H. Lawrence: Symbolic Landscapes
D.H. Lawrence: Infinite Sensual Violence
Rimbaud: Arthur Rimbaud and the Magic of Poetry
The Ecstasies of John Cowper Powys
Sensualism and Mythology: The Wessex Novels of John Cowper Powys
Amorous Life: John Cowper Powys and the Manifestation of Affectivity (H.W. Fawkner)
Postmodern Powys: New Essays on John Cowper Powys (Joe Boulter)
Rethinking Powys: Critical Essays on John Cowper Powys
Paul Bowles & Bernardo Bertolucci
Rainer Maria Rilke
Joseph Conrad: *Heart of Darkness*
In the Dim Void: Samuel Beckett
Samuel Beckett Goes into the Silence
André Gide: Fiction and Fervour
Jackie Collins and the Blockbuster Novel
Blinded By Her Light: The Love-Poetry of Robert Graves
The Passion of Colours: Travels In Mediterranean Lands
Poetic Forms

POETRY

Ursula Le Guin: Walking In Cornwall
Peter Redgrove: Here Comes The Flood
Peter Redgrove: Sex-Magic-Poetry-Cornwall
Dante: Selections From the Vita Nuova
Petrarch, Dante and the Troubadours
William Shakespeare: Sonnets
William Shakespeare: Complete Poems
Blinded By Her Light: The Love-Poetry of Robert Graves
Emily Dickinson: Selected Poems
Emily Brontë: Poems
Thomas Hardy: Selected Poems
Percy Bysshe Shelley: Poems
John Keats: Selected Poems
Joh n Keats: Poems of 1820
D.H. Lawrence: Selected Poems
Edmund Spenser: Poems
Edmund Spenser: Amoretti
John Donne: Poems
Henry Vaughan: Poems
Sir Thomas Wyatt: Poems
Robert Herrick: Selected Poems
Rilke: Space, Essence and Angels in the Poetry of Rainer Maria Rilke
Rainer Maria Rilke: Selected Poems
Friedrich Hölderlin: Selected Poems
Arseny Tarkovsky: Selected Poems
Arthur Rimbaud: Selected Poems
Arthur Rimbaud: A Season in Hell
Arthur Rimbaud and the Magic of Poetry
Novalis: Hymns To the Night
German Romantic Poetry
Paul Verlaine: Selected Poems
Elizaethan Sonnet Cycles
D.J. Enright: By-Blows
Jeremy Reed: Brigitte's Blue Heart
Jeremy Reed: Claudia Schiffer's Red Shoes
Gorgeous Little Orpheus
Radiance: New Poems
Crescent Moon Book of Nature Poetry
Crescent Moon Book of Love Poetry
Crescent Moon Book of Mystical Poetry
Crescent Moon Book of Elizabethan Love Poetry
Crescent Moon Book of Metaphysical Poetry
Crescent Moon Book of Romantic Poetry
Pagan America: New American Poetry

MEDIA, CINEMA, FEMINISM and CULTURAL STUDIES

J.R.R. Tolkien: The Books, The Films, The Whole Cultural Phenomenon
J.R.R. Tolkien: Pocket Guide
The *Lord of the Rings* Movies: Pocket Guide
The Cinema of Hayao Miyazaki
Hayao Miyazaki: *Princess Mononoke*: Pocket Movie Guide
Hayao Miyazaki: *Spirited Away*: Pocket Movie Guide
Tim Burton : Hallowe'en For Hollywood
Ken Russell
Ken Russell: *Tommy*: Pocket Movie Guide
The Ghost Dance: The Origins of Religion
The Peyote Cult
Cixous, Irigaray, Kristeva: The *Jouissance* of French Feminism
Julia Kristeva: Art, Love, Melancholy, Philosophy, Semiotics and Psychoanalysis
Luce Irigaray: Lips, Kissing, and the Politics of Sexual Difference
Hélène Cixous I Love You: The *Jouissance* of Writing
Andrea Dworkin
'Cosmo Woman': The World of Women's Magazines
Women in Pop Music
HomeGround: The Kate Bush Anthology
Discovering the Goddess (Geoffrey Ashe)
The Poetry of Cinema
The Sacred Cinema of Andrei Tarkovsky
Andrei Tarkovsky: Pocket Guide
Andrei Tarkovsky: *Mirror*: Pocket Movie Guide
Andrei Tarkovsky: *The Sacrifice*: Pocket Movie Guide
Walerian Borowczyk: Cinema of Erotic Dreams
Jean-Luc Godard: The Passion of Cinema
Jean-Luc Godard: *Hail Mary*: Pocket Movie Guide
Jean-Luc Godard: *Contempt*: Pocket Movie Guide
Jean-Luc Godard: *Pierrot le Fou*: Pocket Movie Guide
John Hughes and Eighties Cinema
Ferris Bueller's Day Off: Pocket Movie Guide
Jean-Luc Godard: Pocket Guide
The Cinema of Richard Linklater
Liv Tyler: Star In Ascendance
Blade Runner and the Films of Philip K. Dick
Paul Bowles and Bernardo Bertolucci
Media Hell: Radio, TV and the Press
An Open Letter to the BBC
Detonation Britain: Nuclear War in the UK
Feminism and Shakespeare
Wild Zones: Pornography, Art and Feminism
Sex in Art: Pornography and Pleasure in Painting and Sculpture
Sexing Hardy: Thomas Hardy and Feminism

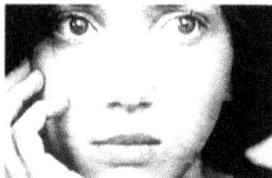

The Light Eternal is a model monograph, an exemplary job. The subject matter of the book is beautifully organised and dead on beam. (Lawrence Durrell)
It is amazing for me to see my work treated with such passion and respect. (Andrea Dworkin)

CRESCENT MOON PUBLISHING
P.O. Box 1312, Maidstone, Kent, ME14 5XU, Great Britain. www.crmoon.com

cresmopub@yahoo.co.uk   www.crescentmoon.org.uk